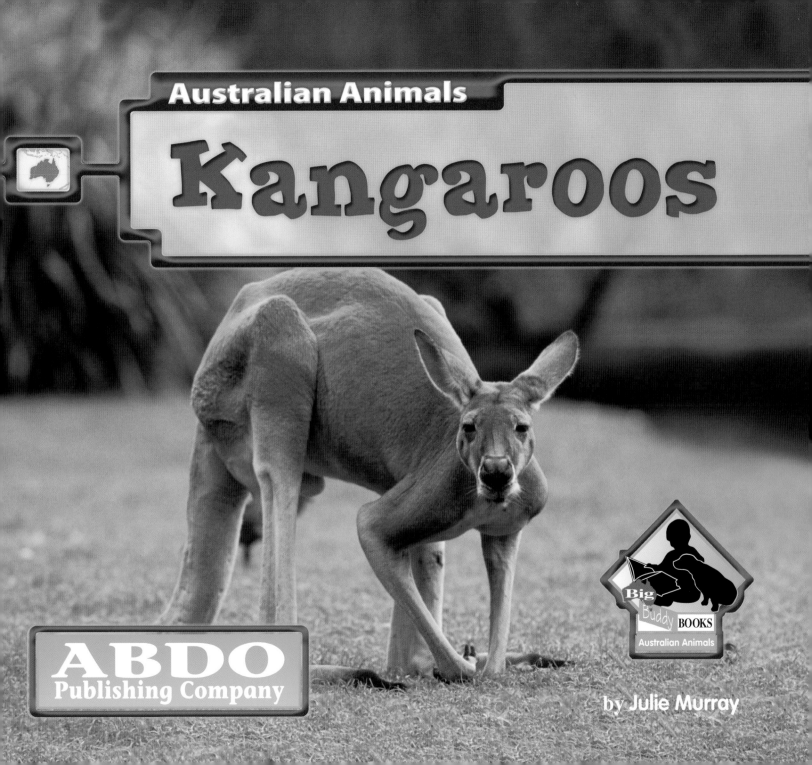

Australian Animals

Kangaroos

ABDO
Publishing Company

Big Buddy BOOKS
Australian Animals

by Julie Murray

VISIT US AT

www.abdopublishing.com

Published by ABDO Publishing Company, 8000 West 78th Street, Edina, Minnesota 55439.

Copyright © 2012 by Abdo Consulting Group, Inc. International copyrights reserved in all countries. No part of this book may be reproduced in any form without written permission from the publisher. Big Buddy Books™ is a trademark and logo of ABDO Publishing Company.

Printed in the United States of America, North Mankato, Minnesota.
052011
092011

♻ PRINTED ON RECYCLED PAPER

Coordinating Series Editor: Rochelle Baltzer
Editor: Marcia Zappa
Contributing Editors: Megan M. Gunderson, BreAnn Rumsch, Sarah Tieck
Graphic Design: Maria Hosley
Cover Photograph: *iStockphoto*: ©iStockphoto.com/twildlife.
Interior Photographs/Illustrations: *AnimalsAnimals - Earth Scenes*: Patti Murray (p. 27), Alan Root/OSF (p. 25),
    S. Turner/OSF (p. 27); *Corbis* (p. 7); *iStockphoto*: ©iStockphoto.com/aleskramer (p. 11), ©iStockphoto.com/
    arjayphotography (p. 13), ©iStockphoto.com/carolgaranda (p. 12), ©iStockphoto.com/cbpix (p. 9), ©iStockphoto.
    com/CraigRJD (p. 15), ©iStockphoto.com/eeqmcc (p. 20), ©iStockphoto.com/Gurilla (p. 11), ©iStockphoto.
    com/hddigital (p. 9), ©iStockphoto.com/JohnCarnemolla (pp. 11, 19), ©iStockphoto.com/Keiichihiki (p. 5),
    ©iStockphoto.com/markrhiggins (p. 10), ©iStockphoto.com/Matejay (p. 4), ©iStockphoto.com/MaXPdia (p. 17),
    ©iStockphoto.com/nanookbrent (p. 25), ©iStockphoto.com/robynmac (p. 29), ©iStockphoto.com/RuslanDashinsky
    (p. 29), ©iStockphoto.com/TimothyBall (p. 4); *John Foxx Images* (p. 19); *Shutterstock*: Kitch Bain (p. 23).

Library of Congress Cataloging-in-Publication Data

Murray, Julie, 1969-
 Kangaroos / Julie Murray.
   p. cm. -- (Australian animals)
 ISBN 978-1-61783-011-2
 1. Kangaroos--Juvenile literature. I. Title.
 QL737.M35M87 2012
 599.2'22--dc22
                            2011002298

Contents

Long ago, nearly all land on Earth was one big mass. About 200 million years ago, the land began to break into **continents**. One of these is an island called Australia.

Kangaroos are known for hopping on their powerful back legs.

Living on an island allowed Australian animals to **develop** separately from other animals. So today, many are unlike animals found anywhere else in the world! One of these animals is the kangaroo.

Kangaroo Territory

There are six types of kangaroos. The three main types are red, eastern gray, and western gray kangaroos.

Red kangaroos live in the center of Australia. This area is called the outback. It is mainly desert and dry grasslands.

NORTHERN TERRITORY

WESTERN AUSTRALIA

QUEENSLAND

SOUTH AUSTRALIA

NEW SOUTH WALES

VICTORIA

TASMANIA

▦ Red Kangaroo Territory

Australia's outback is mostly wild. Very few people live there. Red kangaroos make the outback their home.

Uncovered!
Kangaroos belong to a large family of related animals. It includes wallabies and tree kangaroos.

Eastern gray kangaroos live in eastern Australia and on the island of Tasmania. Western gray kangaroos live on the southern part of the **continent**. In these places, gray kangaroos live mostly in forests. They go into grasslands to eat.

NORTHERN TERRITORY

QUEENSLAND

WESTERN AUSTRALIA

SOUTH AUSTRALIA

NEW SOUTH WALES

VICTORIA

Western Gray Kangaroo Territory

Eastern Gray Kangaroo Territory

TASMANIA

Gray kangaroos usually live in wet parts of Australia. There, rain helps their favorite foods grow.

Uncovered!
Australia is completely surrounded by water. That is why many people call it the island continent.

Welcome to the Continent Down Under!

If you took a trip to where kangaroos live, you might find…

INDIAN

West-Australian Basin

...English.

Most Australians speak English. But, some words are different from the English spoken in the United States. For example, in Australia a sweater is called a jumper. And, a cookie is often called a biscuit. Australians also have different names for kangaroos. Females are called does, jills, and flyers. Males are called bucks, jacks, and boomers.

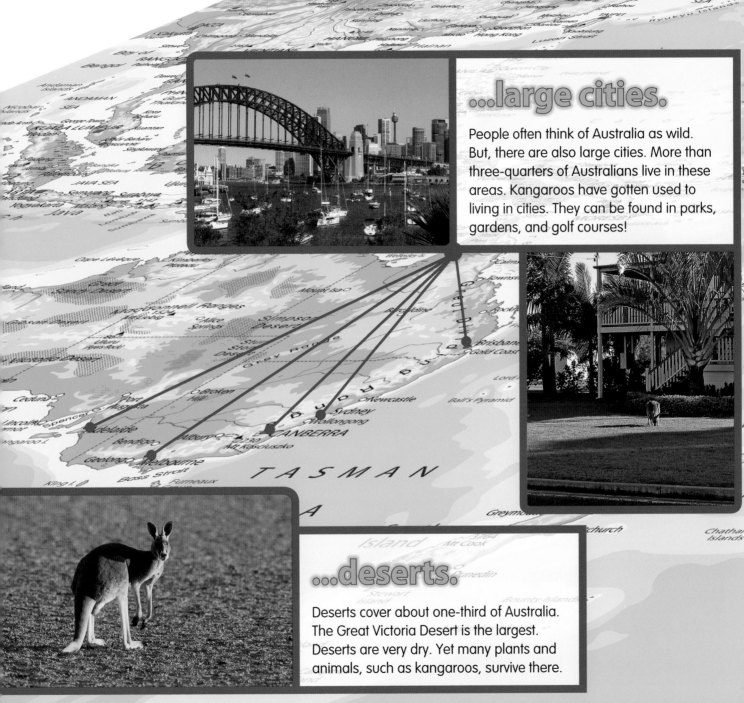

...large cities.

People often think of Australia as wild. But, there are also large cities. More than three-quarters of Australians live in these areas. Kangaroos have gotten used to living in cities. They can be found in parks, gardens, and golf courses!

...deserts.

Deserts cover about one-third of Australia. The Great Victoria Desert is the largest. Deserts are very dry. Yet many plants and animals, such as kangaroos, survive there.

Take a Closer Look

Kangaroos have small heads with large ears. They have short front legs and large, powerful back legs. Kangaroos have sharp claws. They also have long, strong tails.

Kangaroos are covered in thick, **rough** fur. They can be reddish, brown, bluish, or gray.

Kangaroos lean on their tails for support when they rest.

A kangaroo can turn its
ears to listen for danger.

Kangaroos are different sizes. Red kangaroos can be up to six feet (1.8 m) tall. They weigh almost 200 pounds (90 kg)!

Gray kangaroos can be up to seven feet (2.1 m) tall. Eastern gray kangaroos weigh about 130 to 200 pounds (60 to 90 kg). Western gray kangaroos weigh about 120 pounds (55 kg).

Kangaroos have big feet. They may grow up to 18 inches (46 cm) long!

Hopping About

A kangaroo's back legs cannot move separately. So, kangaroos move by hopping on both feet at the same time. They use their large tails to stay balanced.

Kangaroos can hop very fast. Some can move more than 35 miles (56 km) per hour for a short length. And if scared, kangaroos take giant leaps. They can hop 6 to 10 feet (1.8 to 3 m) high and more than 25 feet (8 m) away in one jump!

Uncovered!
Moving by hopping on two back legs is called saltation (sal-TAY-shuhn).

To increase speed, kangaroos don't hop faster. Instead, they take longer leaps. This helps keep them from tiring out.

Mob Scene

Kangaroos often eat, sleep, and travel together in groups called mobs. A kangaroo mob is led by one powerful male.

Male kangaroos often fight one another to become the leader. They lean back on their strong tails. Then, they hit or kick each other with their legs.

When kangaroos hit each other, it is called "boxing."

In the outback, kangaroo mobs often gather at watering holes.

Kangaroos **communicate** with each other in many ways. This includes giving meaningful looks, fighting, and cleaning each other. Kangaroos also grunt, cough, hiss, and click.

Kangaroos look out for other members of their mob. They warn them of danger by thumping their feet on the ground.

Mealtime

Most kangaroos eat early in the morning or just before nighttime. They rest during midday when it is hottest.

Kangaroos are herbivores (HUHR-buh-vawrs). This means they eat plants. Red and gray kangaroos eat mostly grasses.

Kangaroos can **survive** for long periods of time without water. This allows them to live in dry areas like Australia's outback.

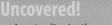

Uncovered!
Australia is the second-driest continent after Antarctica.

When eating, kangaroos move slowly on all four legs. They use their tails for balance.

Baby Roos

Kangaroos are part of a group of **mammals** called marsupials (mahr-SOO-pee-uhls). Marsupials have tiny babies called joeys.

Joeys are born before they are done **developing**. A newborn joey lives inside a special pouch on its mother's belly. There, it continues growing.

Uncovered!
Koalas, wombats, and opossums are also marsupials. There are more than 250 kinds of marsupials. Most are native to Australia.

Kangaroos are the most common type of marsupial in Australia.

A newborn kangaroo joey is only about one inch (3 cm) long. It cannot see or hear.

Female kangaroos usually give birth to one joey at a time. A newborn kangaroo joey crawls inside its mother's pouch. There, it drinks its mother's milk and grows.

After six to ten months, a joey comes out of its mother's pouch. It begins to eat grasses. It returns to the pouch again and again until it is too big.

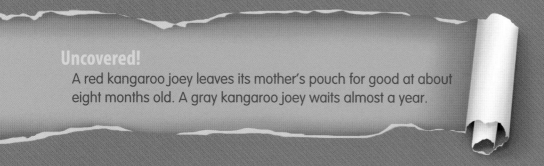

Uncovered!
A red kangaroo joey leaves its mother's pouch for good at about eight months old. A gray kangaroo joey waits almost a year.

As a joey gets bigger, its head and feet stick out of its mother's pouch.

If a joey is hungry, tired, or scared, it dives headfirst into its mother's pouch!

Survivors

Kangaroos face many dangers. Wild dogs called dingoes hunt them for food. Some people kill them for their meat, for their skin, or for sport. New buildings take over their **habitats**. And, food can be hard to find during **droughts**.

Still, kangaroos **survive**. Today, millions of them live in Australia. Kangaroos help make Australia an amazing place!

Uncovered!

The Australian government protects kangaroos. It takes special care of types that are in danger of dying out.

28

Dingoes are tough enemies. But, kangaroos bite, kick, and scratch to protect themselves.

Kangaroos in the wild can live from six to more than 20 years!

Crikey!
I'll bet you never knew...

...that kangaroos can't walk backward.

...that a kangaroo joey poops and pees in its mother's pouch! Its mother has to clean it out.

...that long ago, giant kangaroos lived in Australia. An adult giant kangaroo grew about six and a half feet (2 m) tall. It weighed up to 500 pounds (230 kg)! Giant kangaroos died out within the last 100,000 years.

...that kangaroos belong to the family Macropodidae. This Latin word means "big feet"!

Important Words

communicate (kuh-MYOO-nuh-kayt) to share knowledge, thoughts, or feelings.

continent one of Earth's seven main land areas.

develop to go through steps of natural growth.

drought (DRAUT) a long period of dry weather.

habitat a place where a living thing is naturally found.

mammal a member of a group of living beings. Mammals have hair or fur and make milk to feed their babies.

rough (RUHF) not smooth.

survive to continue to live or exist.

Web Sites

To learn more about kangaroos, visit ABDO Publishing Company online. Web sites about kangaroos are featured on our Book Links page. These links are routinely monitored and updated to provide the most current information available.

www.abdopublishing.com

Index